The Official

Chelsea FC Annual 2009

A Grange Publication

ISBN 978-1-906211-31-8

£6.99

Contents

Introduction

We really hope you enjoy this year's Official Chelsea Annual. When Chelsea signed up manager Luiz Felipe Scolari we dumped the 'High School Musical' soundtrack and worked along to Brazilian samba CDs instead.

When José was here we already picked up some football phrases in Portuguese. Felipe will obviously be impressed that we can already shout for handball ('Mão na bola!'), a foul ('Falta!'), and say 'unlucky' ('Infeliz') to the opposition – very useful after Chelsea has beaten them!

Inside you'll find some great pictures and stories from last season and even further back in Chelsea's history, as well as the usual quizzes, facts and stats.

In fact, we're almost as excited about the new Annual as we are about the 2008/9 season. (Almost, but not quite.)

Enjoy them both!

SEASON RE

The Special One departs.

A frustrating draw at home to Norwegian team Rosenborg in the Champions League was the last match for José Mourinho at Chelsea. He left Stamford Bridge soon after and was replaced by director of football Avram Grant.

It was another season to remember, but always for the best reasons.

Memories of th

City stunned at the Bridge.

Michael Essien whacked in Chelsea's first agains
high-flying Man City as October came to a clos
Sven Goran Erikkson's men were well beaten 6-
and Chelsea were on fire.

Lamps makes light work of 100 goals.

In February Frank scored in the FA Cup against Huddersfield to complete a century of goals for Chelsea since his arrival in June 2001. What an amazing record for a midfielder!

VIEW

That comeback at home to Arsenal.

Nicolas Anelka came on as a sub with Chelsea trailing 0-1 against Arsenal, and helped Didier Drogba destroy the Gooners. It finished 2-1, with the Drog grabbing both goals - and celebrating like a madman.

2007/8 season

Beating our record at Upton Park.

When Ashley Cole scored his first goal for Chelsea it was our fourth against West Ham at their home, Upton Park. And that's our biggest ever win in the east London stadium.

Those 4-4 draws.

Well, they weren't the result we wanted but you can't argue that they were boring! Incredibly, we drew 4-4 with both Aston Villa and Spurs. On Boxing Day Michael Ballack thought he'd earned all three points against Villa. But in injury time Ashley Cole stopped a shot on the line and Gareth Barry scored the penalty. Lightning struck again in March when Joe Cole (pictured) scored late on. But Robbie Keane pounced with two minutes remaining to level the scores.

SEASON RE

Hitting Derby for six.

Lamps grabbed a hat-trick in March as we hit six past Derby County. We scored eight against them home and away, with only one goal in reply

VIEW

Knocking Liverpool out of Europe at last.

The Scousers had enjoyed all the luck whenever we'd met in the Champions League but in this season's semi-final the turning point was probably John Arne Riise's own goal at Anfield. After that 1-1 result, Chelsea confidently saw them off 3-2 at the Bridge to reach the final for the first time in our history.

eating the Mancs.

ichael Ballack slammed home his second goal a penalty – to beat Manchester Utd 2-1 and eep alive Chelsea's hopes of winning the remier League. In the end we finished close second, which was a wonderful erformance from the squad after so any injuries and other problems. Well done lads!

A great experience in Moscow.

We didn't win the game, but we won lots of new friends around the world for how well we played, and – apart from Lamps's brilliant equaliser – the highlight of the evening was Petr's wicked save from Ronaldo's penalty. It was a wonderful trip but it won't be our last Champions League final.

Joey can't wait!

Skilful winger Joe Cole grew up in Camden and joined Chelsea from West Ham in 2003. He recovered from injury to have one of his best ever seasons for England and the Blues, and was named our Player of the Year. Here's what he's thinking about the new season.

On accepting his award for Player of the Year...

'It was really nerve-wracking up there. I could see the faces of everybody in the audience and although I have played in some fantastic stadiums in the past, in front of thousands of people, I have never had to speak to them like then.'

On what the award means...

'I am really proud to have won this award as it is voted for by the fans and I'd like to dedicate it to them.'

Joe was a Chelsea supporter as a boy and one of his favourite players was Dennis Wise.

On the new manager...

'I'm getting a good vibe from him. It is early days but he seems very approachable and has a huge football pedigree. I'm really excited to play for him. Everyone is optimistic and it is exciting for Chelsea.'

On looking forward to playing for Luiz Felipe Scolari...

'The way he sets his teams up, I've been waiting for it my entire career - a manager who wants to play the right way. I'm nearly 27 now, and have been waiting for someone like him to come along. He already has the respect of the boys and has settled in nicely. I think it's going to be happy days for everyone.'

On Scolari's previous work...

'From what I know about the way Mr Scolari set up Portugal and Brazil, and watching them play, it was beautiful football. There are plenty of players who like to get the ball down, I'm so excited.'

On having a holiday instead of playing at Euro 2008...

'I went to Barbados, Las Vegas and Florida, and had a really good break. I had four weeks off doing nothing, which is a long time for any footballer, but for an international it is an awful long time.'

And on how Chelsea might benefit from England players having a rest...

'When you look at it that way you expect all the English players to hit the ground running in the season, so that's good news for Chelsea, but also teams like Man United who have a strong English core.'

On what the fans mean to him...

'Football pundits can criticise you and make judgements on the way you play, but they don't watch you every week like fans do. What they think is really important to me.'

And now Youth got to believe us!

It is not just the first team at Stamford Bridge that is making history. In April 2008 a Chelsea Academy team became the first to reach an FA Youth Cup final since 1961. Here's what happened.

> "Everyone at the club was delighted the team got to the Final." Chelsea chief executive Peter Kenyon.

In the early rounds of the competition, Chelsea staged home matches at Griffin Park, where the club's reserves usually play. In the fourth round against Shrewsbury, attacking left-back Patrick van Aanholt was among the scorers in an impressive 4-0 win.

Adam Phillip scored a vital equaliser in the semi-final first leg against a tough and well-organised Aston Villa side to take a 1-1 draw to the away rubber. Phillips specialised in coming off the bench to score in the competition.

Chelsea fought hard to win 3-2 at Villa Park in the second leg of the semi, with France Under-17 international Gaël Kakuta scoring the Young Blues' second after a brilliant 50-yard solo run. They had reached the final at last.

Huge crowds turned up at Stamford Bridge for the home legs of the semi-final and final. Entry was free and the fans really got behind the young stars.

The Youth Cup champions would be crowned after the second leg at SportCity. Chelsea were up against it, facing a very strong Manchester City team after

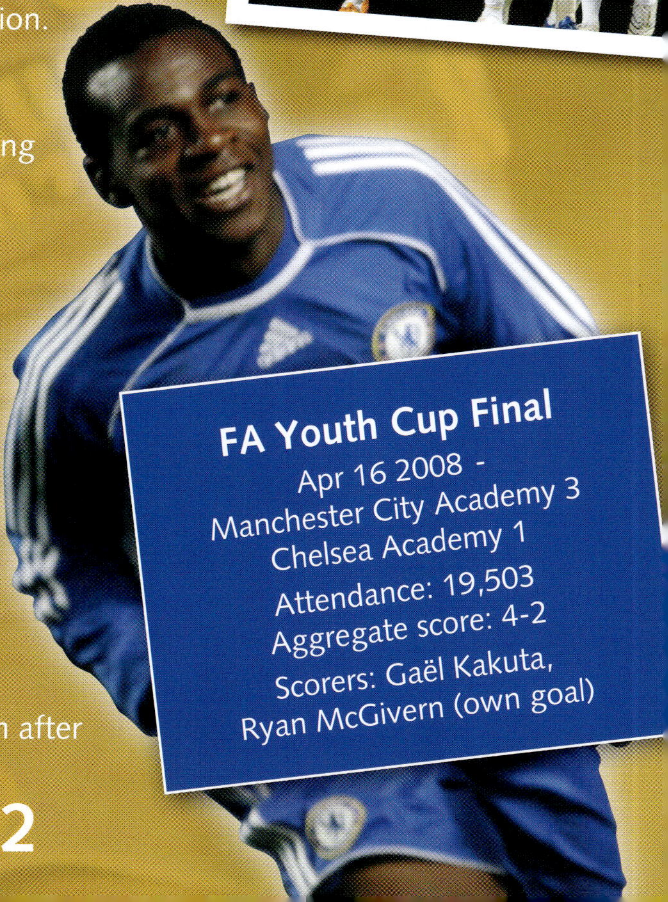

FA Youth Cup Final

Apr 16 2008 -
Manchester City Academy 3
Chelsea Academy 1
Attendance: 19,503
Aggregate score: 4-2
Scorers: Gaël Kakuta,
Ryan McGivern (own goal)

STAR PLAYER: GAËL KAKUTA

Date of birth: Jun 21 1991

It's harsh highlighting just one player from such great team performances, but the attacking midfielder from Lille, France has everything and shows it. Pace, tricks, a great shot and, most of all, amazing awareness of what pass to play makes this left-footer one to watch. Kakuta signed professional forms with Chelsea in July after his 17th birthday.

managing a 1-1 at the Bridge. An own-goal by a City defender, after good work by Jacob Mellis, was all Chelsea had to show for some excellent play, and as Chelsea looked for goals City hit them on the break to win 3-1 – 4-2 on aggregate. It was a fantastic effort by all the lads, though, and Luiz Felipe Scolari will be watching their progress with interest in the coming years. Well done to Paul Clement, Chelsea's Youth Team manager. He was the man who steered the lads to a first Youth Cup final for the club in 47 years.

ROUTE TO THE 2008 FA YOUTH CUP FINAL
Dec 13 2007 – Stevenage Academy 0 Chelsea Academy 1 Scorer: Adam Phillip
Jan 17 2007 – Chelsea Academy 4 Shrewsbury Town Academy 0 Scorers: Jacob Mellis (2), Patrick van Aanholt, Michael Woods
Jan 31 2008 – Chelsea Academy 3 Leicester City Academy 1 Scorers: Morten Nielsen, Gaël Kakuta, Miroslav Stoch
Feb 26 2008 – Port Vale Academy 2 Chelsea Academy 5 Scorers: Gaël Kakuta (3), Morten Nielsen, Miroslav Stoch
Mar 7 2008 - Semi-final 1st leg: Chelsea Academy 1 Aston Villa Academy 1 Scorer: Adam Phillip
Mar 19 2008 - Semi-final 2nd leg: Aston Villa Academy 2 Chelsea Academy 3 Scorers: Sergio Tejera, Gaël Kakuta, Adam Phillip

Michael Essien & Joe Cole

Luiz Felipe Scolari

Who's going to make it...

1,000 Premier League goals!

At the start of the 2008/9 season Chelsea had scored 977 goals in the Premier League, going right back to 1992/3. The Blues usually score well over 23 goals each season, so someone is going to make history by grabbing the 1,000th.

CURRENT PLAYERS IN OUR ALL-TIME TOP 30 PL SCORERS*	
Frank Lampard	71
Didier Drogba	50
Joe Cole	23
John Terry	16
Salomon Kalou	14
Michael Ballack	12
Andriy Shevchenko	9

Make a note here of your predictions of who will score and when.

It will be scored by: ______________ Against: ______________

And it will be a [penalty/header/free kick/left-foot shot/right-foot shot/own goal]

Frank Lampard is Chelsea's all-time top Premier League scorer with 71 goals. Sixty of the 977 goals before this season have been from the penalty spot. Twenty-nine of the 977 were own goals. The only person to have scored own goals with two different clubs is Colin Hendry (Coventry and Bolton).

We've put together some facts to help you decide.

PREMIER LEAGUE SCORERS (977)

Frank Lampard	71 (16 pens)
Jimmy Floyd Hasselbaink	69 (12 pens)
Gianfranco Zola	59 (1 pen)
Eidur Gudjohnsen	54 (2 pens)
Didier Drogba	50
Gustavo Poyet	36 (1 pen)
John Spencer	36 (2 pens)
Tore André Flo	34
Dennis Wise	33 (6 pens)
Mark Hughes	25 (1 pen)
Joe Cole	23
Mark Stein	21 (3 pens)
Gianluca Vialli	21 (1 pen)
Hernán Crespo	20
Frank Lebœuf	17 (10 pens)
Gavin Peacock	17
Dan Petrescu	17
John Terry	16
Roberto Di Matteo	15
Arjen Robben	15
Damien Duff	14
Salomon Kalou	14
Paul Furlong	13
Michael Ballack	12 (2 pens)
William Gallas	12
Michael Essien	10
Mick Harford	9
Andriy Shevchenko	9 (1 pen)
Graham Stuart	9
Craig Burley	7
Jesper Grønkjær	7
Eddie Newton	7
Neil Shipperley	7
Mario Stanic	7
Ricardo Carvalho	6
Tony Cascarino	6
Sam Dalla Bona	6
Marcel Desailly	6
Adrian Mutu	6
Frank Sinclair	6
Celestine Babayaro	5
Mikael Forssell	5
Bjarne Goldbæk	5
David Lee	5 (1 pen)
Jody Morris	5
Carlton Cole	4
Gérémi	4
Ruud Gullit	4
Mateja Kezman	4 (1 pen)
Graeme Le Saux	4
Mario Melchiot	4
Scott Minto	4
Tiago	4
Andy Townsend	4
Shaun Wright-Phillips	4
Boudewijn Zenden	4
Mal Donaghy	3
Robert Fleck	3
Gareth Hall	3
Glen Johnson	3
Mark Nicholls	3
George Weah	3
Alex	2
Darren Barnard	2
Juliano Belletti	2
Laurent Charvet	2
Jon Harley	2
Paul Hughes	2
Jacob Kjeldbjerg	2
Bernard Lambourde	2
Claude Makelele	2
Florent Malouda	2
Emmanuel Petit	2
Claudio Pizarro	2
Nicolas Anelka	1
Wayne Bridge	1
Pierluigi Casiraghi	1
Ashley Cole	1
Steve Clarke	1
Assier Del Horno	1
Michael Duberry	1
Glenn Hoddle	1
David Hopkin	1
Erland Johnsen	1
Vinnie Jones	1
Andy Myers	1
Scott Parker	1
Chris Sutton	1
Juan Sebastián Verón	1
<u>Own goals</u>	<u>29</u>
Henning Berg	2 (Man Utd)
Colin Hendry	2 (Coventry & Bolton)
James Beattie	1 (Southampton)
Matthew Brazier	1 (QPR)
Sol Campbell	1 (Tottenham)
Martin Crainie	1 (Southampton)
Nikos Dabizas	1 (Leicester)
Richard Dunne	1 (Man City)
Ugo Ehiogu	1 (Aston Villa)
Matt Elliott	1 (Leicester)
John Fashanu	1 (Wimbledon)
Rio Ferdinand	1 (West Ham)
Alain Goma	1 (Fulham)
Ivar Ingimarsson	1 (Reading)
Jussi Jaaskelainen	1 (Bolton)
Zurab Khizanishvili	1 (Blackburn)
Chris Kirkland	1 (Wigan)
Dominic Matteo	1 (Leeds)
Lilian Nallis	1 (Leicester)
Gary Pallister	1 (Middlesbrough)
Dean Richards	1 (Southampton)
Liam Rosenior	1 (Fulham)
Richard Shaw	1 (Crystal Palace)
Frank Sinclair	1 (Leicester)
Michel Vonk	1 (Man City)
Sander Westerveld	1 (Liverpool)
Abel Xavier	1 (Middlesbrough)

* Figures correct as at 31 July 2008

www.chelseamegastore.com

BUY DIRECT, SUPPORT YOUR CLUB

The Official Online Megastore for UK/Europe
+44 (0) 871 231 0005
calls from a landline will cost a maxiumum of 10p per min, mobiles rates may vary

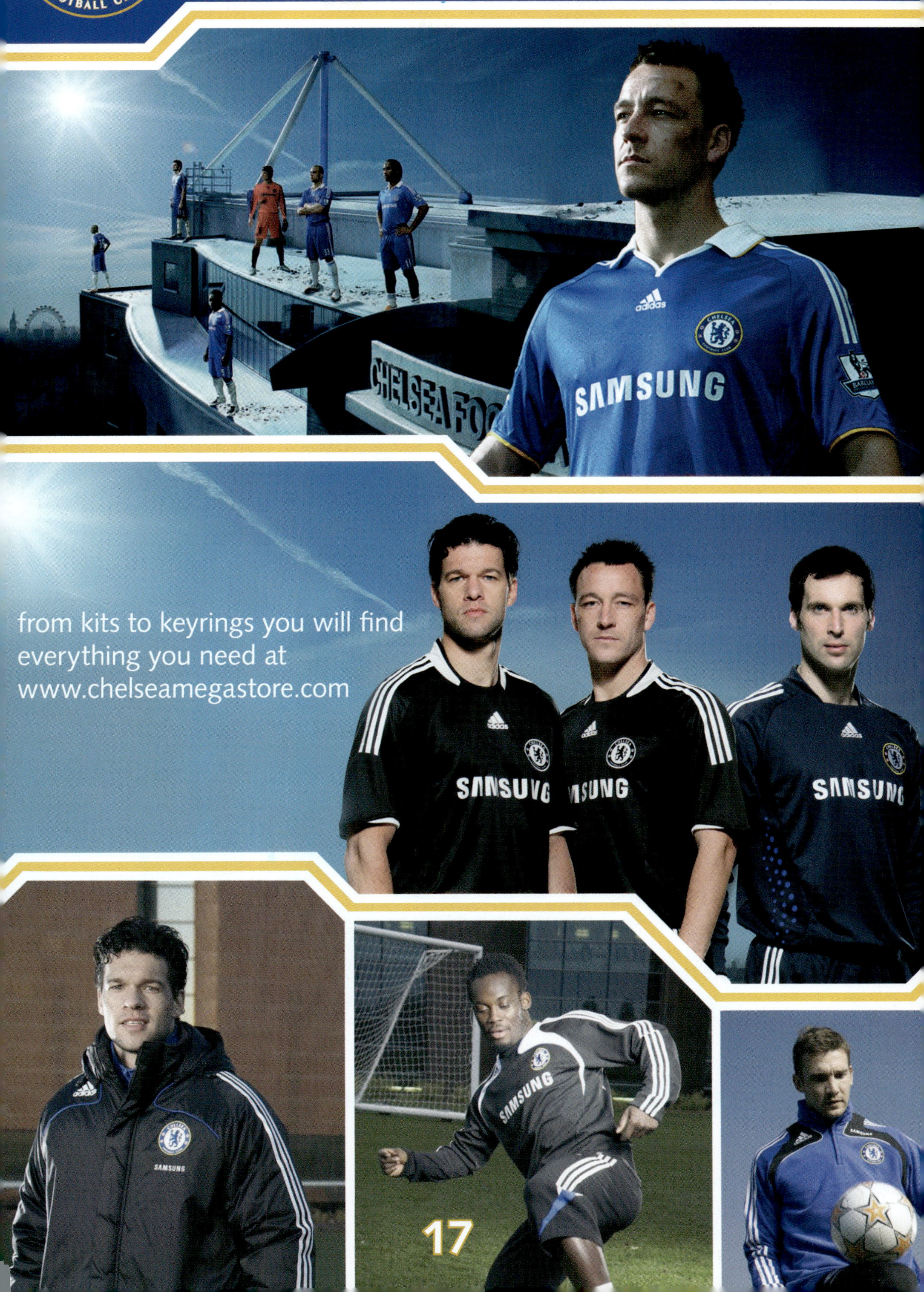

Ashley Cole

is looking forward to playing like an attacking Brazilian wing-back.

Networks:	**Chelsea FC, England**
Birthdate:	20 December 1980
Hometown:	Stepney, London, United Kingdom
Squad Number:	3

Michael Ballack

was arguably Chelsea's best player in the last third of the season – the Kaiser is back!

Networks:	**Chelsea FC, Germany**
Birthdate:	26 September 1976
Hometown:	Chemnitz, Germany
Squad Number:	13

John Terry

Chelsea and England's inspirational captain.

Networks:	**Chelsea FC, England**
Birthdate:	7 December 1980
Hometown:	Barking, London, United Kingdom
Squad Number:	26

Petr Cech

is buzzing about the new manager and determined to help Chelsea win even more silverware this season.

Networks:	**Chelsea FC, Czech Republic**
Birthdate:	20 May 1982
Hometown:	Plzeň, Czech Republic
Squad Number:	1

Franco di Santo

is a fantastic young striker with a killer instinct in front of goal.

Networks:	**Chelsea, Argentina**
Birthdate:	7 April 1989
Hometown:	Mendoza, Argentina
Squad Number:	9

Deco

is one of the best in the world at opening up opposition defences with a killer pass.

Networks:	**Chelsea, Portugal**
Birthdate:	27 August 1977
Hometown:	Sao Bernardo do Campo, Brazil
Squad Number:	20

Salomon Kalou

has just got back from the Olympic Games and is raring to go.

Networks:	**Chelsea, Ivory Coast**
Birthdate:	5 August 1985
Hometown:	Oume, Ivory Coast
Squad Number:	21

Wayne Bridge

has signed a new contract and is a Chelsea stalwart.

Networks:	**Chelsea, England**
Birthdate:	5 August 1980
Hometown:	Southampton, Hampshire, United Kingdom
Squad Number:	18

José Bosingwa

is a lightning fast attacking right-back who will make a big impact in his debut season at the Bridge.

Networks:	**Chelsea, Portugal**
Birthdate:	24 August 1982
Hometown:	Kinshasa, Democratic Republic of Congo
Squad Number:	17

Carlo Cudicini

is one of Chelsea's longest-serving players, and would probably start every game at any other club.

Networks:	**Chelsea, Italy**
Birthdate:	6 September 1973
Hometown:	Milan, Italy
Squad Number:	23

Henrique Hilario

is the superbly reliable understudy to Petr and Carlo.

Networks:	**Chelsea**
Birthdate:	21 October 1975
Hometown:	São Pedro da Cova, Portugal
Squad Number:	40

Joe Cole

is going to enjoy himself playing for a Brazilian manager.

Networks:	**Chelsea, England**
Birthdate:	8 November 1981
Hometown:	Romford, Essex, United Kingdom
Squad Number:	10

Michael Essien
is the brilliant, unstoppable force in Chelsea's midfield.

Networks:	**Chelsea, Ghana**
Birthdate:	2 December 1982
Hometown:	Accra, Ghana
Squad Number:	5

Paulo Ferreira
is reunited with his national team boss Luiz Felipe Scolari.

Networks:	**Chelsea, Portugal**
Birthdate:	18 January 1979
Sex:	Male
Hometown:	Cascais, Portugal
Squad Number:	19

Branislav Ivanovic
had a good pre-season and will look forward to competing for a regular first team place.

Networks:	**Chelsea, Serbia**
Birthdate:	22 February 1984
Hometown:	Sremska Mitrovica, Serbia
Squad Number:	2

Didier Drogba
is probably the greatest striker in the world!

Networks:	**Chelsea, Ivory Coast**.
Birthdate:	11 March 1978
Hometown:	Abidjan, Ivory Coast
Squad Number:	11

Nicolas Anelka
put four past AC Milan in pre-season and is enjoying his new, more direct role under Scolari.

Networks:	**Chelsea, France**
Birthdate:	14 March 1979
Hometown:	Versailles, France
Squad Number:	39

Scott Sinclair
is young and improving all the time.

Networks:	**Chelsea, England**
Birthdate:	25 March 1989
Hometown:	Bath, Somerset, United Kingdom
Squad Number:	16

Mikel John Obi
is going to have a big season now that Maka has left Chelsea's midfield.

Networks:	**Chelsea, Nigeria**
Birthdate:	22 April 1987
Hometown:	Jos, Nigeria
Squad Number:	12

Ricardo Carvalho
has probably been Chelsea's best player over the last two seasons.

Networks:	**Chelsea, Portugal**
Birthdate:	18 May 1978
Hometown:	Amarante, Portugal
Squad Number:	6

Florent Malouda

has a season in England under his belt and has the touches to worry any defence.

Networks: **Chelsea, France**
Birthdate: 13 June 1980
Hometown: Cayenne, French Guiana
Squad Number: 15

Alex

takes the the wickedest long-distance free kicks.

Networks: **Chelsea, Brazil**
Birthdate: 17 June 1982
Hometown: Niteroi, Brazil
Squad Number: 33

Juliano Belletti

only knows how to score the most amazing goals.

Networks: **Chelsea, Brazil**
Birthdate: 20 June 1976
Hometown: Cascavel, Brazil
Squad Number: 35

Frank Lampard

has scored 20 goals in each of his last three seasons, and will probably do so again.

Networks: **Chelsea, England**
Birthdate: 20 June 1978
Hometown: Romford, Essex, United Kingdom
Squad Number: 8

Juliano Belletti
35

CHELSEA FOOTBALL CLUB
SAMSUNG
Frank Lampard

Alison and Stamford

Your Chelsea TV series is hugely popular. What do you think gives the show such appeal?

Alison: Well that's got to be down to Stamford. The young fans (and adults!) love him. He can't go anywhere without being stopped for photographs – he loves it though! I also think 'Skill School' is fantastic. There aren't many places where you can get taught by the same person who trains our future Chelsea stars.

Stamford: Yes 'Skill School' is one of my favourites too. With so many skills to be learnt there is rarely a chance to 'paws' for thought.

What are the most fun parts to film?

Alison: It's all good fun as we are just having a laugh, but it's most enjoyable when we get invited on location. I loved filming at the Natural History Museum because I hadn't been there since I was a kid and it brought back some great memories. The T. Rex was terrifying: I genuinely jumped when he roared. (Do dinosaurs roar? Maybe I've been hanging out too much with Stamford!)

Stamford: Yes the T. Rex scared me too – I thought he was going to chase me all the way back to Stamford Bridge! That was almost as frightening as the time Alison convinced me to go to the gym.

Which of the 'Mini Motty' performances has been the most memorable for you?

Alison: There have been so many great ones, the future of English commentary is in good shape: watch out Motty! I loved the kid who said Kaaaaaalllllllllllllloooooooooooouuuuuuuuuuuuuuuuu. He was great.

Stamford: Alison keeps promising me that I can have a go soon. I like to think I will be the next Brian Roar. Get it?! [I think he means the old commentator Brian Moore – Ed.]

They co-host one of Chelsea TV's most popular shows, but how do they really get along? Roaringly, as we found out!

We all love 'Skill School', but who's the best at tricks among the Chelsea lads?

Alison: Probably the most skilful is Joe Cole but he doesn't tend to do that many tricks in training. I love watching him play though.

Stamford: Joe is also one of my favourites. I also love watching the youth team train. Those lads are extremely skilful and I can't wait for some of them to break into the first team.

On skills, do you have a secret non-football one you'd like to share with us?

Alison: I used to be a breakdancer and I can still spin on my head! Maybe one week I'll teach Stamford.

Stamford: Alison always tries to copy my disco dancing. My 'moonwalk' in the Chelsea Museum one time was particularly pleasing.

Stamford, who is your favourite opposition team mascot?

Stamford: I like Harry the Hornet at Watford. We grew up together and he used to live in my ear when I was a cub.

Alison, Chelsea players apart, who do you think is the dishiest footballer around?

Alison: Ha ha! Giving away my secrets... can I have two? They are both Spanish and far too young for me, but Fernando Torres and Sergio Ramos are my top two! Sorry to pick a Liverpool player, but I've liked him since he was with Atlético!

Finally, any tips to would-be TV stars reading this?

Alison: Be keen, work hard, even unsociable hours, and be prepared to start from the very bottom earning very little money! Sometimes you'll still be working at 4am on a Saturday morning and thinking, 'What am I doing?' But if you don't give up you'll get to where you want to be. These days it helps to be multi-skilled, so it's good to have a solid background in written journalism and TV production too.

Stamford: Be nice to people that you work with and treat everybody with respect. But the biggest thing is to have fun and enjoy what you do.

39
BALLACK
13

CHELSEA
FOOTBALL CLUB
adidas

BLUE SAID THAT?

Once again everyone has been talking about Chelsea, but it does not always make sense. Can you work out who made the following comments about the Blues? Answers are on pages 60.

1. "The idea is to play our game as similar as Brazil in football, but I have English football players and the character of each player is different."

2. [After Chelsea had beaten his team 4-0 at home] "If you took the goals out of it, I think it was pretty even."

3. "Nothing surprises me in football, but if I said I was astounded that would be an understatement."

4. "It is a relief to get to the 100-mark because I was on 99 and then I got injured."

5. "If Chelsea are naive and pure then I'm Little Red Riding Hood."

6. "The fans in Britain don't miss me more than I miss them, for sure. Chelsea was a beautiful period of my career."

Go behind the scenes at Chelsea FC!
Take the tour of Stamford Bridge and visit areas of Chelsea Football Club that you would have only ever dreamed of seeing!
adidas
SAMSUNG
• See your favourite players' shirts hanging in the amazing home dressing room
• Walk out of the tunnel onto pitchside and hear the roar of the crowd
• Take a seat 'on the bench' in the dugouts
• Sit in the press room and see what it's like to give your own press conference
• Learn about the rich history of the Blues in the new Chelsea FC Museum
CECH
TERRY
26
SAMSUNG
CHELSEA FOOTBALL CLUB
MUSEUM AND STADIUM TOUR
To book call 0871 984 1955
r visit www.chelseafc.com/tours
or more information
ll tours are subject to availability, alteration or cancellation without prior notice. Stadium Tours and
useum will be closed on all home Matchdays and the day before home Champions League games.

ROLL OF HONOUR 2007/8

– CHELSEA'S AWARD WINNERS

This year's Chelsea awards evening was staged in a grand hall under the West Stand at Stamford Bridge, and as usual the gongs were handed out for Player of the Year, Samsung Players' Player of the Year, Young Player of the Year, Outstanding Achievement and Goal of the Season.

Player of the Year: Joe Cole.

Popular Joe, a childhood Blues fan, is so popular he might have won this award before, but this season there was a landslide poll for the midfielder – especially in votes cast on the internet. Joe was all the happier to have returned from a long lay-off with such strong performances, especially in the middle part of the season.

'I played a lot of football this year,' he said as he accepted his trophy, 'which I haven't for a while, because I got injured last season and missed most of the season. I've enjoyed it. I think it will only be the best year if there's some silverware on the table.'

'I voted for Wisey [Dennis Wise] when I was a kid. I loved him when he was at Chelsea so it feels strange to have my name on the trophy next to his.' Player of the Year Joe Cole

Goal of the Season: Juliano Belletti.
It doesn't get much better than scoring Chelsea's goal of the season – against arch-rivals Spurs! The Brazilian's magnificent 30-yard scorcher was voted the best of the bunch, and his similar goal at Wigan was not far behind it. Not bad for a right-back, el

'I saw the space and tried to sho because I saw it was possible that I could score. I had time t prepare the ball and my body so the shot was just right.' Scorer of the Goal of the Seas Juliano Belletti

Samsung Players' Player of the Year: Ricardo Carvalho.
Riccy was one of the closest rivals to Joe Cole's Player of the Year award. The hugely popular Portuguese centre-back was Chelsea's outstanding defender. He was introduced by former Blues legend Ray Wilkins (right).

Special Recognition Award: John Dempsey.
He was one of the stars of Chelsea's UEFA Cup-Winners' Cup final victory over Real Madrid in 1971. Now he's making a big difference in the lives of people with disabilities. Both ways he's a hero, and the club honoured former defender John with a special award.

Outstanding Achievement: Frank Lampard.
Amazingly, Super Frank reached the 100 goals mark for Chelsea in 2007/8, and scored 20 per season three times on the trot. A true Chelsea legend.

'I voted for Joe Cole this year. He has been in excellent form and is a worthy winner. He is a great Chelsea player.' All-time highest Chelsea goalscorer Bobby Tambling

'oung Player of the Year: he Chelsea Youth Cup Team.
kipper Nana Ofori-Twumasi accepted he award on behalf of all his team- nates. In 2008 they became the first Chelsea side to reach the FA Youth Cup final in 47 years. 'I think it's lovely ecognition for the players,' said team nanager Paul Clement.

Two-time winner of Player of the Year, John Hollins

Previous Chelsea Players of the Year.

This award has been given annually since 1967. Here are the previous winners.

1967 Peter Bonetti
1968 Charlie Cooke
1969 David Webb
1970 John Hollins
1971 John Hollins
1972 David Webb
1973 Peter Osgood
1974 Gary Locke
1975 Charlie Cooke
1976 Ray Wilkins
1977 Ray Wilkins
1978 Micky Droy
1979 Tommy Langley
1980 Clive Walker
1981 Petar Borota
1982 Mike Fillery
1983 Joey Jones
1984 Pat Nevin
1985 David Speedie
1986 Eddie Niedzwiecki
1987 Pat Nevin
1988 Tony Dorigo
1989 Graham Roberts
1990 Ken Monkou
1991 Andy Townsend
1992 Paul Elliott
1993 Frank Sinclair
1994 Steve Clarke
1995 Erland Johnsen
1996 Ruud Gullit
1997 Mark Hughes
1998 Dennis Wise
1999 Gianfranco Zola
2000 Dennis Wise
2001 John Terry
2002 Carlo Cudicini
2003 Gianfranco Zola
2004 Frank Lampard
2005 Frank Lampard
2006 John Terry
2007 Michael Essien

STAMFORD SAYS: GET

'Hey, Stamford here! Chelsea are improving the Junior True Blue membership this season, making it even better to sign up to. There's a new-look Bridge Kids mag, and now a cool website just for you. And the best news is – I'm still Editor-in-Chief!'

ONLINE WITH BRIDGE KIDS

It's brilliant. Chelsea have listened to what young fans wanted and are completely revamping the Junior True Blue package, and it costs just £10. If you become a member, look what you now get!

* As usual, you will get priority access to tickets to see the Mighty Blues before they go on general sale, and a discount from the price too.
* On joining you receive a members' pack with a True Blue certificate signed by the players, a brilliant DVD and a wicked wall chart.
* From 2008/9 you'll also get the amazingly cool Bridge Kids magazine four times a year. It's packed with your fave players, plus footie facts, puzzles, interviews and an awesome comic featuring Chelsea FC's very own … Stamford the Lion.
* What's more, the brand new Bridge Kids website is bursting with the latest Chelsea news, video clips, competitions, games, puzzles, footie skills and an online album of player fact cards. Come back each month to collect the set and complete your album! Check it out right now at:

  www.chelseafc.com/bridgekids
* As a Junior True Blue member, you can unlock an exclusive part of the site that's packed with even more fun stuff!

Have a great season,

Stamford

CHELSEA, CHELSEA, TOP OF THE WORLD!

Meet Joseph Brandon, Chelsea's very own mountain goat supporter, whose hobby is to fly the Chelsea flag at the summit of the world's great mountains. Three years ago Joe, usually to be found in the West Stand Lower section where he is a season ticket holder, got to the top of Africa's highest peak, Mount Kilimanjaro (5892m).

In February 2006, though, Joe took the same Chelsea flag to new heights in the Andes. Aconcagua, in Argentina, is not only the tallest mountain in the western and southern hemispheres, but at 6962m it is loftier than anything outside central Asia.

'I reached the summit the same day we beat Arsenal in the Carling Cup final,' smiles Joe. Out of the 14 who started the ascent, he was one of only four who finished the climb. One of the other climbers was a Manchester United fan.

'He had to be taken off the mountain with mountain sickness,' said Joe. 'So unfortunately his flag never got unfurled, whereas mine did. That was another thing we beat them at that season!'

Now Joe has Mount Everest in his sights. Also known as Chomolungma, this is the world's highest mountain at 8848m – the Champions League for climbers! He is already planning the event and looking for sponsors who'd like to see the blue flag flying higher than ever.

There is another side to his mountain-scaling: Joe raised more than £35,000 for the charity in scaling Aconcagua and has become skilled in finding and organising all sorts of inclusive charitable events. He recently raised £18,000 with a run/cycle/walk event round a Thames Water reservoir.

Season-ticket holder Joe took three weeks off from his job for the Andes trek but prepared all winter for the challenge. 'I was already quite fit from my kung fu,' said Joe, an instructor in the martial art, 'but I trained hard for four months and, I'm glad to say, it paid off.

'The blokes who didn't make it to the top were understandably upset.'

For his next challenge Joe knows planning is more important than ever: 'A lot of charities organise trips to the base camp of Everest,' he says, 'but none seem to go to the summit like I'm planning.' Joe is actively seeking sponsors for his charity climb and can be contacted at joebrandon2004@yahoo.com.

Like Chelsea, Joe is hoping to be top of the world next year.

Everest – tall order!

BLUE HUMOUR

How come Omid is a Chelsea fan?

Omid: Chelsea are my local team (I was raised in Kensington) and after they won the FA Cup in 1970 it seemed extremely cool for me as a five-year-old to see people wearing that royal blue Chelsea shirt. I wanted nothing more than to have one myself. The word 'Chelsea' also had much more of a ring to it than 'Arsenal' which I was sure had a rude word in it.

How old were you when you realised you could make people laugh?

I was six. Our teacher had coconut shells and said, 'If you clomp them together they sound like horses galloping.' Two children had a go and got a round of applause. I did it and got belly laughs. To this day I don't know what I did! I presume I was just very excited when I clomped the coconut shells. I probably thought I was really a horse in those few unfortunate seconds.

Omid has appeared in dozens of films including 'Pirates of the Caribbean III: At World's End', 'The Mummy' and 'Sky Captain and the World of Tomorrow'. He was also the voice of Tiger in 'Over the Hedge'.

'Love Guru' actor and award-winning stand-up comedian Omid Djalili has his own brilliant show on TV. More importantly, he's a through-and-through Blue! We caught up with him in between all those fancy premieres and celebrity lunches!

What's your most vivid memory of being at a Chelsea match?

I travelled away a great deal in the 83-84 season when Chelsea were in the Second Division, and on the last day of the season we had to win away at Grimsby to secure the title and pip Sheff Wed. I remember clearly there were more Chelsea fans in the ground than Grimsby. All around me there were Chelsea fans from Burnley, Blackburn – and Grimsby itself! In fact all the Chelsea fans seemed to have northern accents! It's then I saw Chelsea's true appeal.

There's just something special about the club and it wasn't just us born and bred, true blue in west London, who thought so either. We won that game 1-0 with a trademark Kerry Dixon header and the place went mental. Pat Nevin also missed a penalty but it didn't ruin the party.

I also vividly remember Kerry Dixon's goal at Highbury on the first day of the next season being back in the top flight, and seeing the mass of Chelsea fans go wild in the old Clock End. Chelsea was truly back and it felt so good.

You've acted in some amazing films, such as Pirates of the Caribbean III: At World's End. Have you ever considered sneakily wearing a Chelsea shirt on set?

That's the silliest, most ridiculous question I've ever been given. I would never wear a Chelsea shirt 'sneakily'! I wore my Zola no.25 shirt loudly and proudly on the set of 'The Mummy', 'Gladiator', 'Spy Game' etc.

Kerry – scoring one of Omid's favourite goals at Highbury.

So tell us one of your top showbiz mates who's secretly a Blue... (Maybe Keira Knightley...?)

Actor Brendan Fraser would you believe. There you go: he's been outed.

Which opposition fans give you most stick when you're performing (and why)?

Tottenham and Arsenal fans always give me stick. Don't know why. But when they do give me gyp about Chelsea I have the same comeback for all of them: 'Yeah, next year.' That shuts them up.

What's your view of Felipe becoming manager?

I let out a shout of 'Yes!' when I heard the news. He's very 'Chelsea' I think: a big personality, unpredictable, never afraid to make controversial decisions. With his track record he looks like a man who can promise success. There's a buzz about Chelsea and the appointment of Scolari keeps that buzz a-hummin'. He also looks like Gene Hackman so expect some explosive behaviour. Maybe he's been watching some of Gene Hackman's action films and all!

True Blue Brendan, star of the 'The Mummy' films.

What are your favourite football jokes?

I don't actually know many football jokes but I do like the story of when a (very skilful) player called Frank Worthington skinned a (very hard) Liverpool right-back and scored a goal for Leicester in an FA cup semi-final in 1974. As they were walking back, the Liverpool player, Tommy Smith, said to him in full in ear shot of the referee: 'Do that again and I'll break your legs.' Mr Worthington turned to the ref and said, 'Did you hear that ref?!' and the ref said: 'Yes. I think he was talking to you'!

What do expect from the 2008/9 season?

Definitely some silverware for Chelsea. And hopefully England under Fabio Capello turning a corner. I've been watching Capello a lot recently as a player on ESPN Classics (Channel 442 on Sky) where they re-run old European cup finals and old England games from the '70's and Capello was some player. He reminds me of a cross between Steven Gerrard and Claude Makelele. Strong, comfortable on the ball, tough in the tackle and always bombing forward. Now that's what we want from our national team! Make the team in his own image and - keep it quiet - we just might even see England lift the World Cup in South Africa in 2010.

WORDSEARCH

Chelsea have looked to Brazil for new manager Luis Felipe Scolari, so we thought we'd have a Chelsea-flavoured South American theme for this year's word search. The words go up, down, and diagonally, and the answers are on pages 60.

B	E	L	L	E	T	T	I	L	B	G	R	W	M	R
E	R	B	R	E	D	I	E	N	H	C	S	N	C	S
M	F	A	Z	Y	L	R	L	X	A	L	N	R	C	Y
O	S	R	Z	M	H	N	A	N	W	T	Z	O	P	A
H	A	T	B	I	O	H	I	R	S	L	L	F	R	U
T	R	W	C	R	L	T	Q	A	I	A	K	U	A	G
L	I	Z	E	N	N	R	M	D	R	E	R	R	C	U
B	E	V	T	E	Q	B	E	I	Y	E	X	K	I	R
P	M	O	G	M	A	C	V	T	P	M	V	I	D	U
C	L	R	I	P	O	F	Z	O	A	P	I	L	E	F
R	A	J	Y	M	O	P	M	K	X	T	F	B	L	T
E	P	D	C	R	E	Y	M	W	E	W	M	X	L	J
S	T	X	X	M	V	R	E	H	L	J	M	G	I	K
P	Q	R	M	Y	M	R	G	T	A	J	J	Z	R	T
O	Z	W	K	H	P	I	Z	A	R	R	O	J	D	L

CLUES

ALEX
ARGENTINA
BELLETTI
BRAZIL
CRESPO
DECO
FELIPAO
GREMIO
PALMEIRAS
PERU
PIZARRO
POYET
PRACIDELLI
SAMBA
SCHNEIDER
SCOLARI
TEIXEIRA
THOME
URUGUAY
VERON

CHELSEA KITS
THROUGH THE AGES

Chelsea's latest kits boast the very latest material and snappiest designs. But how have they changed over the club's 103 years? We pick out the best and worst Chelsea kits ever. Which one is your favourite?

The first Adidas kit, 2006-8

In 2006 the Blues agreed a deal for Adidas to provide all their kit. The German company's famous feature on all its apparel is three white stripes, as you can see on the sleeve of Michael Essien's shirt at the launch. The replica version of the kit is made of the same quality material that the players wear. Its amazing fabric helped keep the body cool and reduced sweat. It had a hologram badge so you knew it wasn't a fake. We think it's a classic!

The yellow training top, 1972

This training top, worn below by brilliant left-back Eddie McCreadie, was used by Chelsea at the League Cup final against Stoke City in 1972. The classic lion badge has a star either side of it to mark the two trophies Chelsea had recently won: the FA Cup and UEFA Cup-Winners' Cup. It was designed by Umbro, who used to supply both Wembley-final teams with their kit. Yellow has often been the colour of Chelsea's second choice, or away strip. In 2007/8, Adidas designed a luminous 'electricity yellow' shirt that was very striking – to say the least. Your dad might like to know that a version of this 1972 training top is available at the megastore! Doesn't Eddie Mac look the business in it.

The first ever Chelsea kit

Who better than Willie 'Fatty' Foulke, Chelsea's famous goalkeeper, to model the club's first ever football strip? In those days goalies wore the same colours as outfield players (a rule was later introduced that they had to wear different tops) and in 1905 the shirts were made of rough wool. They were a lighter blue than those of today. It was called Eton blue, and was used because that was the colour the club's President, Lord Cadogan, used for his racehorse jockeys' shirts. The shorts were of white cotton – quite a lot of white cotton when they were made for Foulke. The socks were made from thick black wool. Imagine how soggy they got in wet, muddy weather.

A shirt badge appears...

Manager Ted Drake was always looking for ways to smarten up Chelsea's image, and it was he who decided to put a badge on the team's shirts at the start of the 1960/1 season. As seen on sliding Charlie Livesey here, it was very much like today's, with a lion alongside footballs and Tudor roses. The original idea came from the coat of arms of the borough of Chelsea – even though Stamford Bridge is actually in neighbouring Fulham. The lion changed a lot in the 1980s and when Roman Abramovich took over in 2005, one of the first things he did was switch back to a version of this first Chelsea badge. Well done Roman!

Out go the white shorts...

Tommy Docherty was big admirer of Real Madrid's all-white strip, so when he became Chelsea's manager he opted for all-royal blue except the socks, as you can see on our great winger Peter Houseman, above. Docherty later introduced trendy numbers and vertical stripes on the shorts. They were really exciting back in the Sixties! The shorts and shirt were made of cotton, and until former Blue Frank Blunstone opened his sports shop in Clapham, replica kits were unheard of. Young fans had to sew their hero's number on the shirts themselves – unless they could get someone else to do it! Chelsea always looked dazzling in this kit though.

Another winner ...

The current Adidas strip was used in the last two games of last season: Bolton at home in the league, and the Champions League final. It has a little yellow and the Chelsea name on the collar, and is the traditional blue colour. Compared to the 1905 materials, it is lighter, drier, and more washable. There are also two alternative kits that will be used this season: a yellow one and really tasty black one. Which one of them will be the next one we win silverware in? Hey, why not all three!

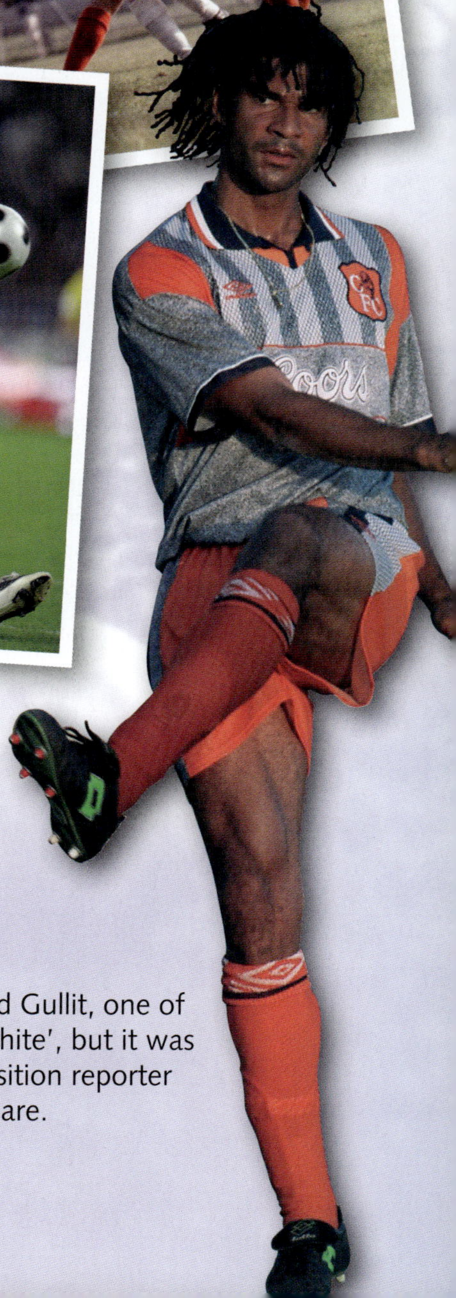

Great players, rotten kit!

Is this Chelsea's worst ever strip? Funnily enough, it is worn here by Ruud Gullit, one of our greatest ever footballers. In 1995 it was billed as 'tangerine and graphite', but it was deeply unpopular. When red-haired Scot David Hopkin wore it, an opposition reporter said Chelsea were playing in camouflage. Thumbs down to a real nightmare.

CHELSEA FC – THE HISTORY

Every week at Stamford Bridge we receive loads of letters from children asking for help with thei school project on the history of Chelsea FC. So we thought we'd provide a useful quick-tips guide to help you on your way to an 'A' grade!

How Chelsea started

There was an athletics ground on the site of Stamford Bridge, Fulham Road, from 1877, surrounded by market gardens. The whole area was bought by Henry Augustus Mears, known as Gus, in 1904. He was a very wealthy sports fan and businessman and did not know whether to turn the land over to houses and shops or build a football ground. Luckily for us he decided on the stadium.

Originally it was supposed to be the new home for nearby Fulham FC, but they changed their mind at the last minute. Gus, his brother Joseph Theophilus and other friends decided to start a football club from scratch.

In 1905 they applied to join the Football League and were elected into the Second Division for the start of the 1905/6 season. No expense was spared on building the "magnificent" new stadium, which held up to 70,000 and had one huge grandstand (where the current East Stand now rests).

Chelsea were an immediately popular attraction. On Good Friday 1906 an amazing 67,000 supporters watched the Second Division game against Manchester United at the Bridge.

They were glamorous too - the famous music-hall entertainer George Robey signed up as a player for a joke. He was the first in a long line of celebrities who continue to support the Blues to this day.

As London's most central club it was regularly visited by the kings of England, Spain and Morocco in the 1910s. The club's shirts were changed to Royal Blue around this time.

Their first nickname was 'The Pensioners', because of the well-known scarlet-jacketed army veterans who live in the nearby Royal Hospital. Although the club changed its nickname to 'The Blues' in 1952, Chelsea Pensioners are still given free tickets for every match at the Bridge.

'The Pensioners', Royal Hospit

Ben Howard Baker 192

Hughie Gallacher 193

Well-known names, but no success

Chelsea signed the first big overseas football star, a Dane called Nils Middelboe, in the 1910s, and a few years later a goalkeeper, Ben Howard Baker, who was a high-jump record holder. Baker used to play basketball with the football around his penalty area!

In the 1930s huge crowds would turn up to see expensive big-name signings like Hughie Gallacher, the greatest centre-forward of his day.

In 1935 a record 82,905 came to see the Chelsea-Arsenal match at Stamford Bridge, a 1-1 draw, with renowned Ireland international, Belfast-born striker Joe Bambrick, scoring Chelsea's goal.

After the Second World War Chelsea spent money again to bring in the famous Tommy Lawton (one of England's greatest ever centre forwards), fellow international forward Len Goulden and Scots star Tommy Walker.

The crowds flocked to the Bridge again, and when Russia's top team Moscow Dynamo visited SW6 in 1945 the Bridge was mobbed by an estimated 100-125,000 fans!

Tommy Lawton 1947

Famous early footballers/personalities

Huge amounts of money were spent buying in players for the new team. The first player-manager, JT Robertson, captain of Glasgow Rangers and a Scotland international, brought in lots of fellow Scots, as well as Irishmen and Welshmen.
Among the few Englishmen was the most famous of that first team: 6'2", 22-stone goalkeeper Willie 'Fatty' Foulke. Foulke was the David Beckham of his day, a very popular figure, partly because his figure was so huge!
One opposition player was told off for missing a penalty against Chelsea, but he complained that Foulke was so big "there was nowhere else to shoot the ball!"
Another early hero was east end Londoner George Hilsdon, who was nicknamed 'Gatling Gun' because his fast, powerful shooting was a like a military weapon.
Hilsdon's image was captured in a weather vane that still stands to this day on top of the East Stand at Stamford Bridge.
Chelsea reached the FA Cup final for the first time in 1915. The Blues lost 0-3 to Sheffield Utd. The match is remembered more for the fact that so many World War I soldiers were present. It was famously called 'The Khaki Final'.

Terry Venables 1959

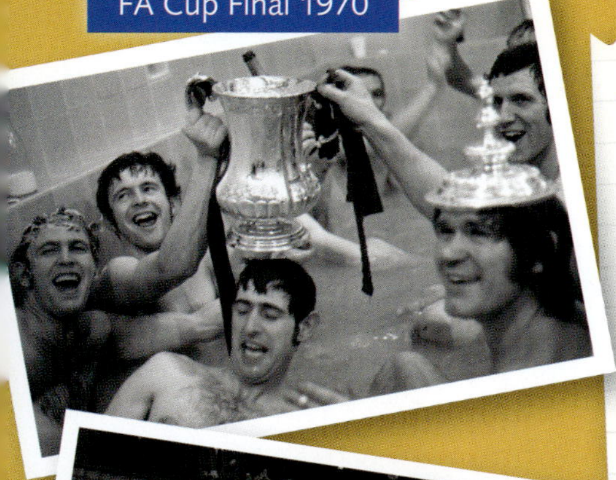

FA Cup Final 1970

Roy Bentley 1955

The first League title

The club changed dramatically in 1952 when manager Ted Drake took over. He made his squad, led by the brilliant Roy Bentley, a centre-forward for England too, super-fit. In 1954/5 Chelsea finally won the Championship for the first time.
Another of Ted Drake's important changes was to produce 'homegrown' players from the Chelsea youth scheme. This produced one of England's greatest ever players – Jimmy Greaves, who in 1958/9 scored 37 goals in one season.
In the 1960s Chelsea teams were made up almost entirely of players who had come through the Blues' Junior scheme.
Peter Bonetti, Terry Venables, Ron 'Chopper' Harris, Bobby Tambling, Peter Osgood and Alan Hudson were just a few of the brilliant players who made Chelsea one of the most attractive and successful teams of the 1960s/70s.
In the late 1960s the Chelsea team came to the fore at the same time that young 'Swinging London' was all the rage. The fashion, art and music of London was the envy of the world, and the King's Road, a few yards from Stamford Bridge, was the centre of Swinging London.
Chelsea, with their stylish, flowing football became known as the 'King's Road Swingers'.
In 1970 Chelsea beat Leeds in a replay at Old Trafford to win the FA Cup for the first time.
The following year they beat the famous Real Madrid to lift the UEFA Cup-Winners' Cup too.

Modern times

In the early 1990s it seemed like Chelsea would have to move out of Stamford Bridge as developers had bought the stadium and wanted to turn it into housing! But new chairman Ken Bates beat off the developers, and a new era soon began for the Blues.

New player-manager Glenn Hoddle brought ambition and modern thinking to the club. He changed players' diets, training, and tactics, and managed to bring in amazing players such as Mark Hughes and Holland and AC Milan's Ruud Gullit.

With Gullit as manager Chelsea reached the 1997 FA Cup final, beating Middlesbrough 2-0. When Gianluca Vialli succeeded Gullit as player-manager, Chelsea won three trophies in 1998 - the League Cup, Cup-Winners' Cup and UEFA Super Cup. Vialli also won the FA Cup in 2000 and Chelsea were looking to become one of the best clubs in Europe.

The biggest change in Chelsea's history came on 1 July 2003, when Russian billionaire Roman Abramovich bought Chelsea FC. Big things were soon to follow for the club.

When new manager José Mourinho arrived, the Portuguese called himself 'a Special One'. Nine months later everyone agreed! In 2005, with Frank Lampard, Damien Duff, Claude Makelele, Petr Cech, Arjen Robben and homegrown skipper John Terry, Chelsea brought the league title back to Stamford Bridge after 50 years.

John Terry went on to become Chelsea's first captain of England since Viv Woodward in 1911.

Roman Abramovich 2003

Rudd Gullit 1997

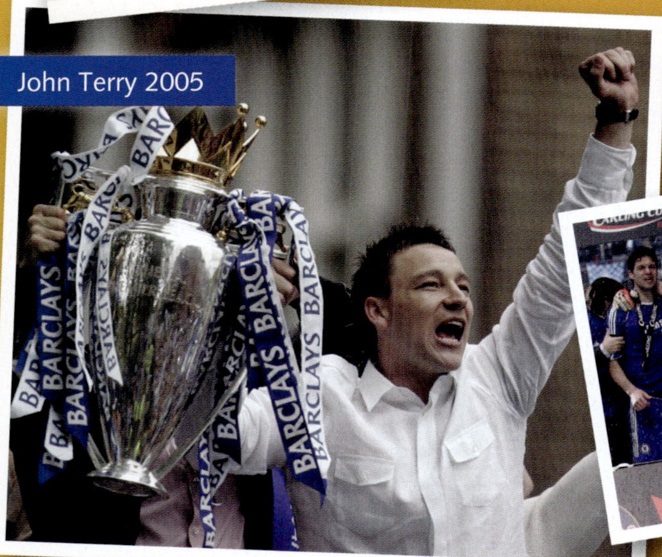

John Terry 2005

League Cup 2007

The team followed up the 2005 success with a second successive Premier League title, and then a domestic double of cup wins – The FA and League Cup - in 2007.

Under next boss, Avram Grant, Chelsea reached a first-ever Champions League final in 2008, where they narrowly lost to Manchester Utd after a penalty shootout.

The current manager is Brazilian Luiz Felipe Scolari. He won the World Cup with Brazil as boss in 2002 and has been in charge of Portugal ever since. His first new signing at Chelsea was the skilful Brazilian/Portuguese midfielder Deco from Barcelona. Are John Terry and Felipe going to bring the league title back to Stamford Bridge? We all certainly hope and believe so!

CROSSWORD

(Answers on page 60)

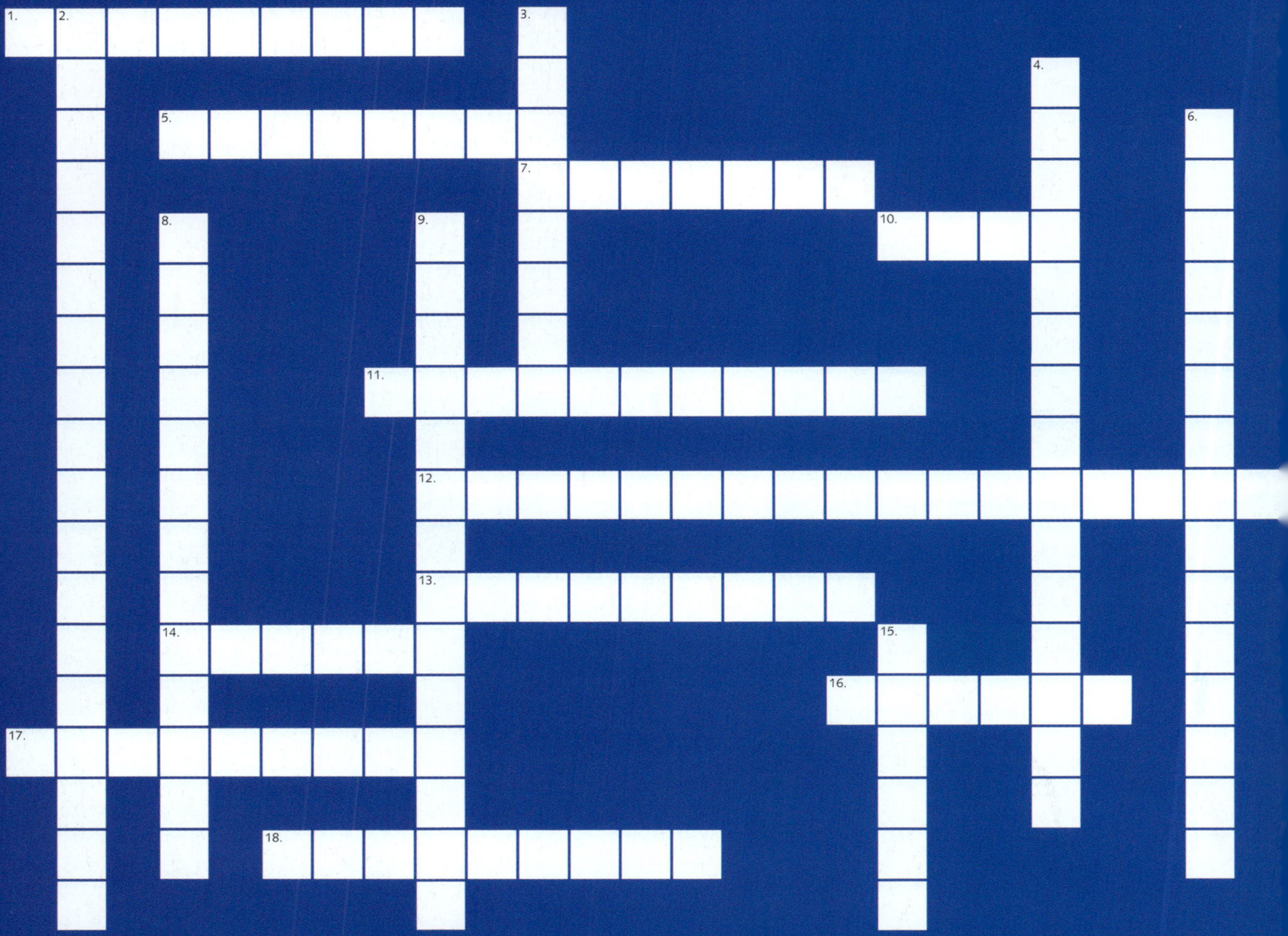

CLUES

Across:

1 Club from whom Chelsea signed Deco (9)

5 What Jose called Michael Essien (3,5)

7 Nationality of defender Branislav Ivanovic (7)

10 Birthplace of Salomon Kalou (4)

11 Luiz Felipe Scolari's favourite book (3,3,2,3)

12 Official name for last year's away shirt colour (11,6)

13 Title of last season's DVD review (4,5)

14 Full surname of John Mikel Obi (6)

16 Where Chelsea played the Champions League Final (6)

17 Team Chelsea beat in last season's Champions League semi-final (9)

18 Chelsea's American chairman (5,4)

Down:

2 February 2008 international tournament featuring Michael Essien, Didier Drogba and Salomon Kalou (6,3,2,7)

3 Home city of Jose Bosingwa (8)

4 The Club's most famous anthem (4,2,3,6)

6 Fans' campaign to make more noise at the Bridge (6,2,3,4)

8 Chelsea's original nickname (3,10)

9 Player who scored the winning penalty against Manchester United in the league (7,7)

15 Location of Chelsea's amazing training ground (6)

SPOT THE BALL!

Use your skill and judgement to work out which lettered ball hides the real one. (Answer on page 61)

Deco

CHELSEA
FOOTBALL CLUB
SAMSUNG
39
John Terry & Nicolas Anelka

CHELSEA'S WEIRDEST

In 103 years a football team is bound to have one or two odd days. But over the years the Blues' players have been shot at, punched and driven back to the dressing room by arctic blizzards. Here are the stories of Chelsea's maddest ever matches…

Two games on the same day.
CRYSTAL PALACE 7 CHELSEA XI 1 – NOV 1905.

Chelsea were vying for promotion from Division Two in their debut season, 1905/6, when the draw for the third preliminary round of the FA Cup produced a visit to Crystal Palace. There was a catch – the game had to be played on the same day as a league fixture against Burnley. Chelsea's first team beat Burnley 1-0 to stay on course for promotion but had to send a complete reserve side across London in the cup – and they were hammered. The FA immediately passed a ruling that forced every team to field a full-strength side in their competition.

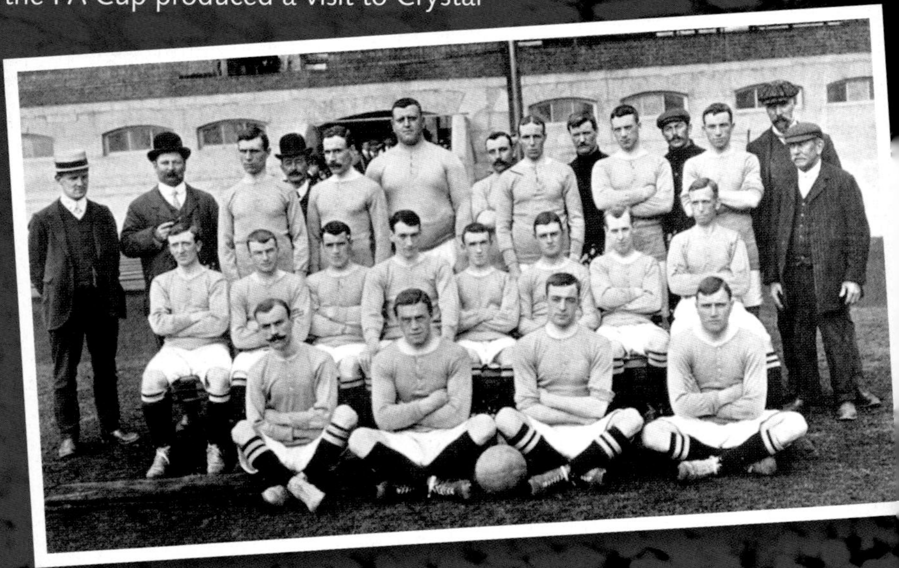

Battered by the seaside.
BLACKPOOL 4 CHELSEA 0 – OCT 1932.

Long before global warming, Chelsea travelled north to play a game in arctic conditions, with driving sleet, freezing wind and a waterlogged pitch on the Lancashire coast. Maybe the Blues were the original southern softies but by half-time, already three goals down, one of our team went off with cramp. Over the break Chelsea's players argued with the ref, and only eight returned for the second half. After Blackpool made it four, two more Chelsea men succumbed to the cold, leaving six on the field. Normally, the match is abandoned if one side has fewer than seven players – but that is always the referee's decision to do so.

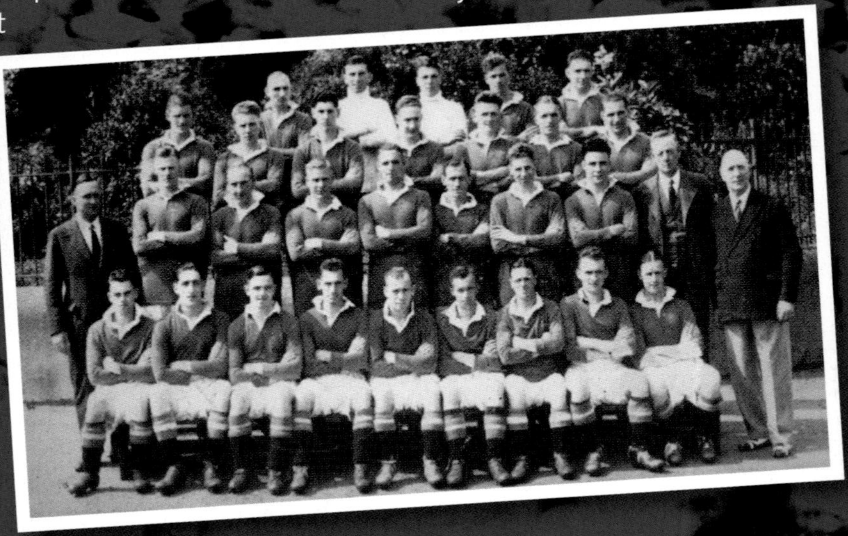

GAMES

The match that was a riot.
CHELSEA 3 MOSCOW DYNAMO 3 – NOV 1945.

Soon after the Second World War had ended, the first-ever visit of a Soviet Union football team took London by storm. So many people were fascinated by what Moscow Dynamo would be like that thousands bunked off work and school and Stamford Bridge was swamped. Locked-out fans climbed walls, trees and nearby houses, the stadium gates broke, and more than 100,000 crammed inside. Supporters had to jump barriers and sit next to the goals for room (see picture). The game has gone down in Chelsea history as one of the greatest ever, but so much damage was done to nearby properties that a court decided a 'riot' had taken place and compensation was paid to our neighbours.

Part-timers put to the sword.
CHELSEA 13 JEUNESSE HAUTCHARAGE 0 – SEPT 1971.

After Chelsea beat the Swiss minnows 8-0 away in the first leg of the Cup-Winners' Cup, striker Peter Osgood (pictured) had a £5 bet with keeper Peter 'The Cat' Bonetti that he would score a double hat-trick against them back at the Bridge. The Jeunesse team – all part-time footballers, and including a one-armed student – were beaten by a scoreline that remains a UEFA record to this day. But when Ossie was on five goals and a penalty was awarded he was denied a sixth when 'The Cat' strolled up and reminded him that John Hollins was the Blues' spot-kick man. Ossie lost the bet and Catty claimed his fiver in the dressing room afterwards.

CHELSEA'S WEIRDEST

The 'Battle of the Bridge'. CHELSEA 4 ROMA 1 1965.

This would have been a remarkable enough game in that it featured a hat-trick from midfield skipper Terry Venables including two brilliantly deceptive free-kicks. Yet it is remembered more for the fighting among players than their brilliance. With Chelsea taking a commanding lead, the Italian visitors got dirty, and the hosts gave it back in equal measure. Venables was stretchered off after one scything tackle, and fiery left-back Eddie McCreadie was sent off for knocking out Carponetti with a right hook. When the Blues arrived for the second leg in Rome the crowd threw missiles throughout the game, despite their coach appealing for calm (pictured). A 0-0 draw secured Chelsea's progress – but Italian fans smashed all windows on the team coach on the way to the airport!

When the shooting wasn't always on the pitch. WISLA KRAKOW 1 CHELSEA 0 – MAY 1936.

You may have heard Chelsea called 'Chelski', and this is the tour of Poland that first earned that nickname way back in 1936. The summer tour also took in Sweden and Holland and was a great success, but the players could probably have done without the over-exuberance of the crowd in Krakow. After centre-forward Harry Burgess (pictured, right) had barged a local player, the Polish supporters took against him and cracks were heard from the terraces. Apparently, when Burgess found himself near team-mate Dickie Spence, the winger said, 'Stay away from me – they're firing shots at you!' The story may or may not be true, but the Second World War was around the corner, and it shows how volatile people considered the mood in Europe was at the time.

GAMES

South American ways.
BUENOS AIRES XI 3 CHELSEA 2 – JUN 1929.

Next year is the 80th anniversary of a landmark overseas tour made by Chelsea in 1929 to Argentina, Uruguay and Brazil. Chelsea became the first English team to wear numbered shirts (and were soon dubbed 'Los Numerados' – see picture), earned many friends and became the first professional British side to play in Sao Paulo. But there were less pleasant moments too. First the locals rejected the footballs that Chelsea had brought with them as too light. At one game they soaked it in a pail of water to make it heavier, then the Argentineans would only allow their own balls to be used. Chelsea chairman Col Crisp was also put out by the South American habit of celebrating a goal with hugs and kisses, and by the bad tempered crowds. Matters came to a head in the match at Boca Juniors' stadium. Firstly Sam Irving was hit with a missile that turned out to be an orange – he calmly peeled it and ate it! Later a challenge by Andy Wilson prompted a mob of supporters to breach a ten-foot fence and attack the visitors. Wilson was punched by a postman, who was arrested by police. But the Buenos Aires skipper, Monti, was far from satisfied, and ran up to the innocent George Roger before punching him on the chin and kicking him in the groin for good measure. Monti was hustled away and the referee abandoned the game with three minutes remaining.

'You only sing when it's snowing!"
TROMSO 3 CHELSEA 2 – NOV 1997.

Venturing into the Arctic Circle is always a challenge, but when manager Ruud Gullit took his Cup-Winners' Cup side to Norway in winter it was something else. Heavy blizzards had created scenes of which Father Christmas and his elves would have been proud and heavy snow restarted during the match. Gullit complained to the UEFA officials again and again but to no avail, and the Tromso players adapted better, racing into a two-goal lead. At several points the pitch markings had disappeared and groundstaff had to sweep the lines regularly. Striker Gianluca Vialli (pictured, far left) was Chelsea's hero, scoring twice to ease fears of an exit. The second leg was duly won 7-1 at the Bridge, 9-4 on aggregate, and Chelsea fans serenaded the disappointed Norwegian supporters who travelled to London: 'You only sing when it's snowing!'

ČECH HIM OUT!

Petr Čech is still the best 'keeper in the world. The big Czech Republic stopper tells all about his homeland, his life and his wicked new Chelsea kit…

On his surname…

'My surname "Čech" means "Czech" in translation. So my situation is similar to that of our doctor at Chelsea, whose name is Bryan English… However, I don't feel like a Czech just because of the surname. I am proud to be Czech and it has always been my dream to play for the national team.

'When I see stuff like "Cech Mate" in headlines here I think it's funny and, if it's done in a good way, I don't mind.'

On his love of chess…

'I actually played chess as a kid and was in competitions when I was seven or eight. When I started playing football I didn't have time anymore. I still quite like it though. I think it's good for relaxing and thinking.'

On his scientifically-tested new goalkeeper's shirt …

'There was a study when I was at Sparta Prague and it said that the perfect colour for the goalkeeper is orange. The striker has only a second to look before he shoots and the orange had a shocking effect. I had the same colour shirt when I was playing for Sparta and we went without conceding for 900 minutes!'

Petr's hero from history.

Karel IV was the powerful eleventh King of Bohemia (born 1316, died 1378). His name is Charles in English, and he was also ruler of Germany, Burgundy, Italy and the Holy Roman Empire. He spoke a number of languages, including French and Czech – just like Petr.

Petr's All-Time World XI

Goalkeeper:
GIANLUIGI BUFFON (Italy, Juventus)

Defenders:
CAFÚ (Brazil, AC Milan), PAOLO MALDINI (Italy, AC Milan),
JOHN TERRY (England, Chelsea) , ASHLEY COLE (England, Chelsea)

Midfielders:
RONALDINHO (Brazil, Barcelona), FRANCESCO TOTTI (Italy, Roma)
CLAUDE MAKELELE (France, PSG, Chelsea), PAVEL NEDVČD (Czech Republic, Juventus)

Forwards:
ANDRIY SHEVCHENKO (Ukraine, Chelsea), RONALDO (Brazil, Real Madrid)

On young Blues fans wearing adidas headguards in his honour...

'It's funny – you can buy my kit but the important part now must be the helmet!

'I really want to see what's going to happen in the future because plenty of kids get knocked out in games where they go a bit crazy and run and jump into everything.

'So maybe if some of the kids feel nervous or not really comfortable diving in at feet, then the helmet can protect them.'

On beating Liverpool to reach the Champions League final...

'After the match I received so many nice congratulations by SMS. A lot of them were sent by my ex-coaches. That was really delightful for me.'

Petr saved Ronaldo's penalty in the Champions League final shootout, but it was not to be. (Background picture)

How to...
eat and drink the Chelsea Way.

From the youngest scholars to the most experienced internationals Chelsea's footballers are given guidance on how to look after their digestive system. Here are a few 100% official dos and don'ts from Chelsea's sports nutritionists.

* Follow the 80/20 Rule: Eat sensibly 80% of the time – leaving 20% to relax. Nothing is 'forbidden', but don't eat much fast food.
* The perfect sports meal has a balance of 'energy' (carbohydrates), 'repair' (proteins) and 'protection' foods (fruit and vegetables).
* Snacking is an important part of the Chelsea Way and helps encourage players to eat little and often. But snack on real food – fruit etc – if possible.
* During exercise no part of the diet is as important as the consumption of water and carbohydrates. Drinking helps prevent declines in concentration and performance. Remaining rehydrated throughout the day will have a positive effect on your health.
* Try this for a footballer's lunch: baked potato, tuna, sweetcorn and diced peppers.
* A good diet will not make a mediocre player a great one, but poor food choices can turn a great player into a mediocre one.
* An excellent evening meal for budding footballers: stir-fried vegetables with beef or chicken strips and noodles.
* Try this as a power breakfast: porridge with half-fat milk, honey and strawberries.

Control your appetite the Chelsea Way by following the rule:

> "I am hungry, I eat –
> I am not hungry, I stop."

PIGMENT POWER – EAT A RAINBOW	
NATURAL COLOUR	**GOOD FOR?**
Blue (eg berry, grape, fig)	Brain
Red (eg tomato, berry, radish)	Energy
Green (eg broccoli, lettuce, kiwi)	Digestion
Yellow/Orange (eg banana, squash)	Skin/eyes
White (eg onion, cauliflower, pear)	Heart

REHYDRATE – STAY FOCUSED

What to drink?	When?
Water & green tea	At all time
Orange juice	At breakfast
Soft drinks	Rarely
Tea & coffee	Sometimes
Sports drink	During exercise only
Milk half-fat	With breakfast cereal and after exercise

live, don't live to eat."

QUIZ ANSWERS

BLUE SAID THAT

Page 30

1 "The idea is to play our game as similar as Brazil in football, but I have English football players and the character of each player is different"

[Answer: **Luiz Felipe Scolari**]

2 [After Chelsea had beaten his team 4-0 at home] "If you took the goals out of it, I think it was pretty even."

[Answer: **Alan Curbishley**]

3 "Nothing surprises me in football, but if I said I was astounded that would be an understatement."

[Answer: **Former Blue - Ray Wilkins**]

4 "It is a relief to get to the 100-mark because I was on 99 and then I got injured."

[Answer: **Frank Lampard**]

5 "If Chelsea are naive and pure then I'm Little Red Riding Hood."

[Answer: **Rafael Benitez**]

6 "The fans in Britain don't miss me more than I miss them, for sure. Chelsea was a beautiful period of my career."

[Answer: **José Mourinho**]

CROSSWORD SOLUTION

Page 48

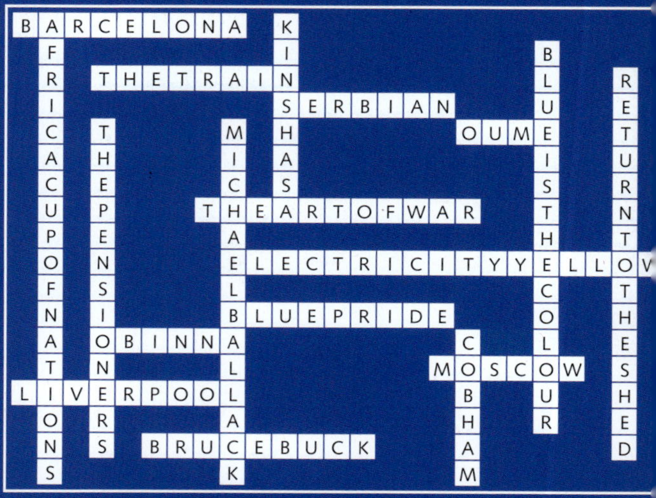

WORDSEARCH SOLUTION

Page 41

QUIZ ANSWERS

SPOT THE BALL

Page 49

The Ecstasy...

Chelsea reached the Champions League final for the first time in the club's history by beating Liverpool in the semi-final, and faced Manchester Utd in Moscow.

Champions League Final
Chelsea 1 Manchester Utd 1
(United win 6-5 on penalties)
Goalscorers: Cristiano Ronaldo, Frank Lampard
Venue: Luzhniki Stadium, Moscow, Russian Federation
Date: 21 May 2008
Attendance: 67,310

Frank Lampard equalised Ronaldo's opening goal on the stroke of half time.

The Blues dominated the second half and extra time, with Frank and Didier beating Van Der Sar only to see their shots rebound off the bar and post (pictured).